FINISHING LINE PRESS

www.finishinglinepress.com

The Dogs of Alishan
and Other Poems from Taiwan

poems by

Laurence Musgrove

Finishing Line Press
Georgetown, Kentucky

The Dogs of Alishan
and Other Poems from Taiwan

Publisher: Leah Huete de Maines
Editor: Christen Kincaid
Cover Art: Ray Mikell
Author Photo: Khrystyna Niewiadomski
Cover Design: Elizabeth Maines McCleavy

Order online: www.finishinglinepress.com
also available on amazon.com

Author inquiries and mail orders:
Finishing Line Press
PO Box 1626
Georgetown, Kentucky 40324
USA

Contents

for Kevin and Steven

Introduction

In June 2023, while in Taiwan on a Fulbright-Hays Seminar Abroad with 15 other scholars from the United States, I drafted the following 13 poems as we attended lectures and toured the island. In a Notes section at the end of this chapbook, I provide an overview of Taiwan, as well as context for each poem and some commentary on their composition.

Taiwan

This island
is a feather
riding upon
a big ocean,
and we crowd
around the long
shaft of its quill
waiting for our
turn to take her
in our hands and
write the glad story
in lasting ink about
the bird and wing
that flew and lost
what we now find
singing softly
inside
us.

Mercy Me

I thought I knew what hot and humid were
Until Taiwan in June which is nothing really
Compared to all I haven't learned yet about
This country where "Power to the People"
Is posted throughout the Presidential Building
We walked through this morning and saw
How many times it was built and destroyed
And restored like so much here on an island
Overrun by so many outsiders again and again,
So I won't waste an undue amount of ink here
On the heat index and instead sit in my hotel
And make mention of my first day in Taipei
And how I plan to return to Longshan Temple
Resurrected from earthquake, fire, typhoon,
And misguided Allied bombs when the golden
Guanyin Buddha alone survived, steadfastly
Listening to our silent cries as we walk within
Her walls and light incense and bow before her
Saying to ourselves, Yes, all will arise again
From quakes, flame, invasion upon invasion,
And even the little mistake I made in ordering
A coffee in the market yesterday, confused by
Another attack of my foreign thoughtlessness
Which I hope to address when I return later
To the herb markets on Xichang Street to taste
The refreshing teas and reflect more coolly
Upon all I invade upon here, all I'd willingly
Empty into the resilient heart of Longshan.

Harmony Tower

As a teen boy in Houston
With the space race on
And rockets standing tall,
I don't now recall the test
I took in what was called

Junior High those days,
But I was tracked for 8
Years of math in just 4,
Yet I was a word kid, not
A numbers one, and sorry

For no exam to determine
Who might enjoy the path
Of art, poetry, music, love,
Or this happy trip to Asia
To marvel at Taipei 101

With its stacked pagoda
(Or is it ancient bamboo?)
Ready to sway in a gale
Or quake because . . . Look!
Up top sits its third eye,

Golden wisdom waiting
To calm and center again,
A weighty lesson for all
When we lose our balance:
Let it dampen the push-pull

Of our confusion and fear
When we feel silenced
And ignored, our gifts
Denied, our leaders blind
To all but their numbers.

Bento

I was today years old (as the saying goes)
When I learned that "brumotactillophobia"
Signifies the obsessive-compulsive disorder
Of a person who absolutely cannot consume
Food on their plate when it touches another
Food on their plate, which is a similar kind
Of illness we find in the United States of
Puritanical Tendencies when the Southern
Baptists decide to purge their pastoral ranks
Of female preachers, a longstanding phobia
Or anxiety generated by the boys club when
They decide the girls are getting too uppity
When they challenge their inability to keep
It in their pants, but what I meant to focus
On is food, and how the Bento lunch boxes
I've been served here in Taipei both reflect
The compartmentalization of food but also
Like every other attempt at categorization
By humankind: noticeable leakage, just like
The border my governor thinks will halt
The refugees or the ancient walls and gates
Here in Taipei but now torn down, replaced
By three-lane roads above the MRT subway
Carrying gladly, calmly, swiftly new friends
And I who have shared across so many tables
So many dishes beautifully prepared, so full
We are of laughter and fellowship, we forget
Where one of us starts and the other one ends.

Bedtime at Sun Moon Lake

On my 3rd-floor balcony at the Shui Sha Lian Hotel in quiet
Shuishe, Yuchi Township, Nantou County, I look down at the
dark boats below at Shuishe Pier and across sleepy Sun Moon
Lake toward Ita Thao where earlier today we moored and
browsed for tea and other indigenous takeaways, when a shop
owner in a dingy shop full of woodcarvings and old statues
spoke into his phone to translate for me the name of some
little porcelain figurines I was smiling at, but I had already
acquired all I planned to tote back to my hotel, including
an exquisite scarf for my wife, (which I'd appreciate you not
telling her about yet so it can be a surprise) but again I worry
too much and see only now how the lights across the water
melt toward me saying, Go to bed, you silly man.

The Dogs of Alishan

Given my completely random
And quite small quantitative study
Of its public canine population,
Likely one quarter is missing
A limb and only one was barking,
But another this morning was singing,
A stout golden retriever with a thick coat
Unlike the small pug and sleek-coated
Hound who knelt in the grass to shit
Near the train station, but I get why
They're here with this air and food,
And the loss of foreleg or rear one
Makes sense what with the razor speed
Of cars and shuttles, especially at night
Here so high so dark, but my favorite
Besides the one of song was an old dog
Lying in the sun this morning, his back
To the closed door of the closed shop,
His right ear up, his left ear down,
Squinting wisely into the warm shine,
Listening to the high song of Alishan.

Chimei Haikuish

Our humble founder
Of performance plastics corp
Plays the violin

And gives all his dough
To install on these manicured
Grounds a replica

(Near half size) of a
European Museum:
Double staircases

And wings and dome tops,
And inside, backpacked children
Follow their teacher.

Magma Speedy Slide

Fulbright-Hays Scholars in Tainan

After waking up in a Cartoon Network Hotel,
we visit Ten Drum Park, another fusion Asian
dish of a morning set in a retired sugarcane
processing plant with archery for the kids,
climbing walls, and Magic Rainbow Train with
Hogswarts-themed flying books and instruments,
and it is also so hot and humid and breezeless,
so I chalk it up to heatstroke when I agreed to
don the requisite helmet, gloves, and squirrel
cape and climb up five flights of rusting stairs
to launch myself down Magma Speedy Slide,
and
     before
        I
           finished
                  asking
              myself
        if it
    was
a smart
        idea,
              I was
                  thumbs up
                      at the bottom.

Crossing from Kaohsiung to Taitung

Resemble
The mind of a traveler,
The flower of chinquapin.
        Basho

The wheels on the bus
Go around and around,
And the scholars in the seats
Sleep or look out their windows
Left and right at mountains
And Hello! there is an ocean,
The Pacific one we flew over
To reach this island Formosa
Where the seven dishes always
(Or is it nine?) arrive in turn,
And surely when the big fish
Is served we will be allowed to
See the end, and someone will
Say OK, EVERYONE! it's time
For a photo, or EVERYONE!
Please meet back here at 3,
Or EVERYONE! it's time to
Get on the bus, and we will be
Counted, and fuzzy-headed
From so much food and heat,
The dragons, lilies, and temples
Still swirling, we climb the steps
Into coolness, we find our seats,
The bus doors whoosh shut,
And the wheels on the bus
Again go around and around.

Anthropocenic Tour

While I'll be 69 this July
In the year Christians
Get to call Twenty 23,
The National Museum
Of Prehistory in Taitung
Reminds us that we sit
As a thin and crispy layer
Atop lots of big numbers
Like the latest estimate
Of our birthday, about 5
Billion years ago, which
Is a run of Twelve zeros,
The amount more than
A few folks these days
Can claim in the bank,
And even the Paiwan
Along the mountains in
The Jinfeng Aboriginal
Township (who can trace
Their Ice Age lineage to
A land bridge from China)
Know the temperature is
Climbing like the plants
Up the slope they must
Follow: banana, millet,
Cassava, elephant ears—
Which they pluck and hold
Over their heads as they
Teach us what's what
Before we all vanish in the heat.

Hualien Haiku

The distillery
of reflection is brewing.
Tourists wait in line.

Along the valley
up from Taitung driving north:
Tropic of Cancer.

The night market glows
near a dark Pacific beach.
Zen tower of stones.

The Portuguese
look up the Liwu River.
Dizem, "Formosa."

KMT veterans
chiseled by hand the highway.
Taroko Gorgeous.

Qixingtan massage
on the hot stones, waves lapping.
Matsu smiles seaward.

Our sightseeing boat
splashes around feeding grounds.
Plume, fin, red lighthouse.

Toto Worship

Parkview Luxury Resort Hotel
Hualien City, Taiwan

It's probably a good thing
We can't read the future
Because I'm not sure we'd like it,
But that doesn't keep us from
Believing that we can create
An improved existence for all
And then build a business strategy
Around that happily-ever-after ending,
Like this Bluetooth toilet
With motion-sensor technology
Waiting patiently for me
In my hotel bathroom
Ready to flip its lid
And light up its bowl
And warm up its seat
So I can sit and poop
While it offers me a menu
Of push-button options
Of cleansing streams and sprays
And bursts of drying air,
All designed for my personal comfort
And improved backdoor hygiene . . .
Hence, I join in the imagining, too:
A new Washlet® app for our phones
To help track all of our movements,
Back massage release assistance,
And customizable retractable footrests
For the most proficient of squatters.

Composition

When the history
Of the island
Is one long
And bloody
Scrolling record
Of terror, tears,
And invasion
By one foreign
Or neighboring
Power after another,
And that island
For a very short period,
Since only 1987,
Finds itself free
Enough at last
To look inward,
(With an eye still
Across the strait!)
That island
Takes the feather
Of itself and under
The white sun
In the blue sky
Plants its flag
In its own red earth.

Notes

This section includes information about Taiwan derived from my notes recorded during the many lectures we attended during this Fulbright-Hays Seminar and other informal research, specifically, geographical, historical, and political contexts for the poems. This Notes section also includes commentary on each of the poems.

Setting. Also referred to as the Republic of China (ROC), the island of Taiwan is separated by a 110-mile strait from the easternmost Fujian Province of mainland China or the People's Republic of China (PRC). Historically, Taiwan has also been referred to as Formosa, which means "beautiful" in Portuguese, the language of one of the island's earliest European explorers.

One of the smallest countries in Asia, Taiwan stands also as the fourth-highest island in the world with a mountainous interior and eastern shore along with an expansive western plain. Taiwan is approximately 95 miles east to west at its widest point and 245 miles north to south. It is commonly described as slightly larger than the state of Maryland and about half the size of Scotland.

Located on the Tropic of Cancer, Taiwan is a subtropical island on the same latitude as central Mexico, Libya, Egypt, United Arab Emirates, Bangladesh, India, Myanmar, and southern China. During June, the daily temperatures reach 90°, and with the high humidity, easily over 100°.

Taiwan also experiences frequent earthquakes: on average, 220 a year of magnitude 4 or greater. Typhoons strike Taiwan about 12 times a year.

Evidence of Taiwan's indigenous population is apparent as far back as 30,000 years ago. After initial Spanish and Dutch settlements in the 17th century and immigration from the mainland thereafter, Taiwan was primarily populated by Han Chinese. The Chinese Qing Dynasty established control in 1683 until its defeat by the Japanese in 1895.

From 1895-1945, Taiwan was a Japanese colony until the Republic of China (ROC), founded in 1912 on the mainland, established its control of the island. Ruled by the ROC's Kuomintang (KMT) political party, Taiwan once again was subject to external authoritarian power.

However, the ongoing Civil War on the mainland between the KMT led by Chiang Kai-shek and Mao Zedong's Chinese Communist Party (CCP) erupted again, and in 1949, the KMT evacuated in defeat to Taiwan with approximately 2 million people, along with significant wealth and cultural artifacts.

The KMT ruled Taiwan via martial law and single-party rule between 1949-1987. This period of fascist persecution is also known as the "White Terror" when more than 100,000 thousand Taiwanese were imprisoned and as many as 4000 executed.

Significant economic growth and political reforms began in the 1960s and 70s, and in 1987, Taiwan transitioned to a representative democracy. Presently, the two main political parties are the Democratic Progressive Party (DPP) and the Kuomintang Party (KMT). The current president is Tsai Ing-wen of the DPP, the first woman to hold that position. In 2017, Taiwan became the first Asian country to legalize same-sex marriage.

Taiwan's free market economy is now the 8th largest in Asia, focusing on electronics manufacturing and communication technology. Taiwan is also one of the largest investors in China's economy with estimates in 2021 near US$200 billion.

Taipei, Taiwan's political, cultural, and economic capital, has a population of 2.5 million and a larger metropolitan population of 7 million. The predominant ethnicity is Han Chinese with a little over 2 percent indigenous peoples encompassing 16 ethnic groups. The official language is Mandarin. 35% of the religious population identify as Buddhist and 33% as Taoist.

Mainland China, or the People's Republic of China (PRC), continues to advance its "One China Principle" which maintains that Taiwan (ROC) has no legitimate nation-state sovereignty of its own. The United States advances a status quo "One China Policy" that does not recognize ROC sovereign nation status while also advancing significant economic ties with both countries and increasing military and political support for Taiwan's identity as an independent democratic nation. Currently, only 13 countries recognize Taiwan's sovereignty. Given the economic power of the PRC, the United States and other major countries in Europe and Asia are not on this list.

In 2020, the U.S. was the largest importer of Chinese products, and China was the third largest importer of U.S. products. In the same year, Taiwan ranked 10th in both U.S. imports and exports.

Introduction. The Fulbright-Hays Seminar Abroad is a U.S. Department of State program within its Bureau of Educational and Cultural Affairs. It is designed to provide U.S. college faculty and staff with a series of presentations and cultural tours in a host country leading to international exchange and curriculum projects that incorporate issues or topics related to that host country into U.S. college courses and programs.

The program of this Fulbright-Hays Seminar began with four weeks (May 10-June 1, 2023) of pre-departure Zoom-mediated lectures led by 15 scholars and organized by the East Asia National Resource Center and the Sigur Center for Asian Studies at The George Washington University.

The in-country program began with our arrival June 6 and departure on July 1, 2023. After a couple days of general sightseeing in Taipei, a series of 20 seminar lectures began on June 9 and continued through June 30, including those by university faculty, secondary school teachers, government officials, political activists, indigenous leaders, and journalists.

During this period, we also toured the island with stops at other cultural sites and major cities, including Sun Moon Lake, Alishan, Chiayi, Tainan, Kaohsiung, Taitung, Taroko Gorge, and Hualien.

My Curriculum Project. I applied for this Fulbright-Taiwan award in 2019 after ending my 10-year stint as department chair. I was granted an alternate award and was told I would receive the full award if someone had to drop out of the program. Due to the COVID-19 pandemic, and the seminar was postponed for 3 consecutive years. In the meantime, someone withdrew their acceptance, and I was notified in March 2023 that I would receive the award.

My original application outlined my interest in the influence of Buddhist culture on education policy and practice in Taiwan. Specifically, I wanted to learn about the pedagogical influence of the Four Noble Truths and the Three Trainings of the Eightfold Path: community, concentration, and compassion.

After the 3-year postponement, this desire continued, evident in my research on Buddhist pedagogy and culminating in an article on the benefits of incorporating Buddhist principles and practices in my English and writing-across-the-disciplines courses: "A Buddhist Educator's Perspective: Well-Being Across the Curriculum."

However, I soon discovered that the pre-departure orientation and the in-country seminar lectures and tours were highlighting politics, geography, economics, social demographics, and history rather than Buddhism and literature. As a result, I revised my curriculum project to focus on contemporary Taiwanese society and culture as a context for understanding its current fiction and poetry.

What I did encounter about Buddhism was revealed in the temples I visited and in a chance meeting with a Fulbright-Taiwan intern, Carrie Chou, a couple of days before I departed. Given what she shared with me (that is, her own experience attending Buddhist schools), I will return to my original plan and investigate the educational mission of the Buddhist Tzu Chi Charity Foundation, especially its university in Hualien, Taiwan.

Tzu Chi, which translates as "compassionate relief," was founded in 1966 by a Taiwanese Buddhist nun, Cheng Yen. Its mission focuses on charity, medicine, education, and humanity, and these are manifested most prominently in medical clinics, schools, and hospitals, as well as international disaster relief efforts and recycling.

Dedication. This chapbook is dedicated to Kevin Chao, our Fulbright-Hays Taiwan tour manager, and Steven Lin, our Fulbright-Hays Taiwan tour photographer. During the length of our 25-day stay, both exhibited unlimited patience and kindness to the 16 of us, wrangling us on and off of buses, ushering us in and out of hotels, conference rooms, and restaurants, and lining us up for one more group photo.

I should also acknowledge here my colleagues at Angelo State University for supporting my application for this award, including Dr. Erin Ashworth-King, Dr. David Bixler, Dr. David Faught, Dr. Karen Cody, Dr. John Klingemann, and Katie Plum.

THE POEMS

Taiwan. This first poem was composed during the first days of our seminar lectures as presenters offered us their perspectives on under-standing the history and culture of Taiwan, as well as its cross-strait tensions with mainland China.

This poem's central image was inspired by one of the presenter's slides which included a feather to represent the shape of the island.

In the background of this poem is also the common Buddhist admonishment that we shouldn't confuse our perspective for the truth: the moon for our finger pointing at it. That doesn't mean that the moon isn't beautiful or that we shouldn't point at it. It only means we shouldn't assume that it's ours to define or fully know. Our knowledge is limited, relative, imperfect, and always a projection of our limited experience rather than some absolute truth.

When I listened to scholars and Taiwanese officials define cross-strait relations between Taiwan and China, or some aspect of history or political achievement, I certainly respected their expertise gained through scholarly study and experience, and I appreciated this new knowledge as it helped me gain a special relationship with Taiwan, but I was also drawn (and this is no criticism) to the distance between their fingers and the moon.

This distance doesn't make their knowing and achievements less important, but let's not confuse ourselves and believe that the ultimate truth is ours to hold and impose. There's enough of that going on in the world already, across the strait, for example, and at home and in any other place where authority is over the moon for itself.

Mercy Me. While I came to Taiwan to learn more about Buddhism, I found instead temple after temple containing an easy mix of Taoist, Confucian, and Buddhist imagery and worship.

I was particularly struck by the many statues of Wenchang Wang, the Taoist God of Culture and Literature, and Guanyin Buddha, a female Bodhisattva associated with Buddhist compassion.

Wenchang Wang, sometimes also referred to simply as Wen, can also be found in temples known as Wen Wu, like the one we visited at Sun Moon Lake, that are dedicated to both Wenchang Wang and Guan Yu, a famous military general; thus, these temples invite worship and veneration on both civil and security matters.

The Longshan Temple mentioned in this poem was built in 1738 by Chinese settlers and contains a variety of deities: Guanyin, Wenchang Wang, Guan Yu, and Matsu, a Chinese sea goddess. Given the importance of fishing to the Taiwanese, Matsu would also be featured prominently in many of the temples we visited, and a large statue of her stood at Qixingtan Beach near Hualien on the northeast Pacific coast of the island.

The Longshan Temple and the Guanyin golden statue in particular have survived a number of natural disasters, such as earthquakes, and Allied bombing during WWII.

Behind this poem was the realization that I had brought to this Fulbright-Hays Seminar a very narrow purpose, and it took a while for me to shake it and to be more open and present to what I was experiencing. In other words, I was invading Taiwan with preconceived ideas about what I wanted to find without attending to what was already there.

Harmony. During our second week in Taipei, a few of our lectures and round table discussions were located in the Grand Hyatt Hotel across the street from Taipei 101, probably the most recognizable landmark in Taiwan, its world trade center. Given frequent earthquakes and typhoons, this building of 101 floors was engineered to be flexible and resilient to these events. Also in support of that balancing act, suspended between its 87th and 92nd floors rests a 660 metric ton pendulum with an 18-foot diameter golden steel ball to offset any structural disturbances.

This poem resonates with my appreciation for this symbol of resilience and forgiveness, a comforting balancing act that helped me feel more settled in the confidence of not exactly knowing what I would learn next from the people I was meeting, the places we were visiting, and the Seminar itself.

The non-reactive mindfulness of Buddhist equanimity is also reflected in this poem.

Bento. Another feature of our second week in Taipei was the onslaught of what I soon came to call "eatin' and meetin'." We would have a couple of lectures in the morning at the Grand Hyatt followed by elegant bento box lunches during the day, more lectures in the afternoon, and then large family-style meals for dinner. These multi-course meals continued through our tour around the island, both lunch and dinner. They provided us with extensive practice in chopstick dexterity and collaborative problem-solving in challenges like, "What Do You That Is?" and "What Number Dish Are We On Now?"

As such, this poem was inspired by the many wonderful meals we shared, and how they allowed us to drop our disciplinary differences and professional personas by moving out of lecture rooms with their front-facing seminar tables into vast dining rooms with their large circular tables passing dishes and serving one another, nourishing friendships in a most congenial way.

Bedtime at Sun Moon Lake. After about 9 days in Taipei, a quick overnight north of town in the Beitou District, a visit to Keelung City, and a hike in Yangmingshan National Park, we took off for a bus tour around the island with our first stop at Sun Moon Lake.

I've got a slow processor of a brain, so I was really beginning to feel the exhaustion of always being on the move. I had to keep reminding myself to keep my patience and humor about me, that we were assigned something equivalent to a fat Norton Anthology Introductory Survey of Taiwan, and I just needed to absorb what I could and dog-ear the pages I wanted to return to later.

Feeling refreshed after a comfortable night's sleep, and on our first morning there, I took a long and pleasant walk with a colleague around the lake to the massive Wen Wu Temple. Afterward, we cooled off in a tea shop near our hotel where I bought three beautiful teapots as gifts to bring back home.

The Dogs of Alishan. One of the highlights of our tour was the highest point we visited: Alishan. We also experienced the coolest temperatures of our tour there with electric blankets waiting on our beds. Elsewhere on the island, normal temperatures during June were in the upper 90s with high humidity equating to at least 110 some days.

In this alpine region, we rose at 3:30 am to board a little train that took us to a trail up the mountain so we could watch the sun rise up over the highest peak in Taiwan at almost 13,000 feet: Yu Shan or Jade Mountain. This train line, constructed during the Japanese colonization era, facilitated the harvest and export of lumber from the region. Currently, Alishan is a little tourist village nestled in the mountains, and that dog really did sing.

This poem also reflects a feeling of homesickness I was beginning to have for my wife and dogs, even though we were video-chatting twice a day via WhatsApp, matching mornings with evenings, evenings with mornings, given the 13-hour difference in our time zones.

Chimei Haikuish. The most peculiar destination was the Chimei Museum in Tainan, and it began an odd series of tour stops that seemed designed for children and their families (rather than adults), including Ten Drum Cultural Village and Hotel Cozzi, a Cartoon Network-themed hotel in Tainan.

The Chimei is a European-styled private museum seemingly plopped down in a huge park with landscaped gardens and fountains just outside of Tainan. Among many examples of Western painting and sculpture, it houses a natural history exhibit, a permanent exhibition of Rodin's work, and the largest violin collection in the world. It also has a 7-11 and Starbucks just inside the main entrance.

Ultimately, the mission of the museum is to offer Taiwanese an introduction to Western art and music, a taste of what they might see in established museums in Los Angeles, Chicago, New York, London, Paris, and Rome.

When sketching a poem in response to this day, I struggled to find a form that would hold and communicate all that we had experienced that day, so I turned to a series of haiku-like stanzas that distill my feelings of being overwhelmed by the pace and the number of stops (and the heat) of our schedule.

Magma Speedy Slide. As I said above, this was an odd day in Tainan, including a tour of a children's amusement park, Ten Drum Cultural Village, which was once a sugarcane refinery. "Magma" is also an apt description of the volcanic heat that day as it radiated off and collected inside the sheet metal silos and other buildings remaining from that refinery and repurposed for the park.

By this time, I had also begun to share my poems with our Fulbright-Taiwan WhatsApp group. Every once in a while, during our excursions, someone would say to me, "This would make a good poem." or "Will you be writing a poem about this?" My identity as tour scribe was soon established, and it motivated me even further to feel less like the English professor outcast among the social scientists.

This poem also reflects my identity as one the oldest participants in our group, which I continually was reminded of when someone offered a hand to me when getting off the bus or said, "Watch your step." or "How are you doing today?" These were welcome kindnesses of course, but my decision to accept the challenge of the Magma Speedy Slide was really the response of a silly old man eager to demonstrate he had some youth and vitality left.

Crossing from Kaohsiung to Taitung. Though our stay in Kaohsiung was one of my favorites—as we toured the port area with its repurposed warehouse district full of restaurants and shops and public art—I was also looking forward to making the turn around the southern end of the island and seeing at last the Pacific to the east.

The epigraph from Basho was inspired by a sudden memory of one of my favorite courses at Southwestern University in Georgetown, Texas, an introductory survey to Asian literature, and I remember how much I enjoyed Basho's haiku and travelogue *The Narrow Road to the Interior*.

The chinquapin referred to in this poem's epigraph is a Japanese chestnut tree, which also represents the happy, resilient, perseverant, and flowering, inspired mind of a traveler.

This poem also serves as a wonderful memory for me of Kevin Chao and Steven Lin, our Fulbright-Taiwan guides, and how our group of scholars were continuing to grow closer during our time together on and off the bus.

Anthropocenic Tour. In Taitung on the east coast, we toured the very excellent National Museum of Prehistory in the morning, and in the afternoon, we visited with members of the Paiwan tribe at a family farm compound in the Jinfeng Township.

This day reminded me of an introductory research and writing course I regularly teach that I've titled "Life and Death on Planet Earth." This undergraduate course is populated by students from a variety of disciplines, and one of the challenges of introductory courses like this is finding a topic that students will find personally engaging, publicly meaningful, and applicable to their fields of study.

In the past, during the pandemic, I selected "immunity" as the topic, we read *On Immunity: An Inoculation* by Eula Biss, and they used this topic and its synonyms as subject terms when conducting research in their own disciplines, terms like "freedom," "protection," "safety," and "infection."

More recently, I selected "extinction" and "climate change" as unifying topics, and I've assigned Elizabeth Kolbert's *The Sixth Extinction: An Unnatural History.* My students have used these and other related terms (death, loss, preservation, and change) in their research.

So, as we toured the museum of Taiwanese prehistory and met with the few remaining members of the Paiwanese indigenous community, Kolbert's book, my students, planetary change, and global warming were forefront in my mind; thus, the title: "Anthropocenic Tour," a reference to the current geological age in Earth's history, the Anthropocene, wherein humans are the primary cause of climate change and extinction events.

Hualien Haiku. Again, I had to resort to haiku stanzas to distill down all I encountered on our way up the east coast and upon our arrival in Hualien, including a rest stop where the Tropic of Cancer crosses the island, a visit to an oceanside night market, a small tower of stones stacked on a dark beach, a hike in Taroko Gorge National Park (where our local tour guide and retired environmental engineer Vincent described how veterans of Chiang Kai-shek's Kuomintang [KMT] National Revolutionary Army carved by hand through the mountains the easternmost section of the cross-island highway), a dolphin-watching, bumpy-splashy boat ride, and a visit to Qixingtan Beach (where Vincent saw me take a break resting comfortably knees up on my back on the hot beach stones and say, "That's a good place for a massage!"). This is also the beach where I found a tall stone statue of Matsu, gazing with a smile out into the Pacific.

The crossing of the Tropic of Cancer mentioned here was another reminder of the heat we experienced. We crossed this subtropical latitude on the day after the Summer Solstice when it sits closest to the Sun just overhead on the longest day of the year.

Toto Worship. This poem's original title was "The Toilets of Taiwan." Of the many wonders of this amazing tour abroad were the elegant hotels that hosted our stays around the island, including most notably the Asia Pacific Hotel in Beitou, Maison De Chine in Chiayi, Cozzi in Tainan (the Cartoon Network-themed hotel), the Indigo Central Park in Kaohsiung, the Naruwan Galaxy Hotel in Taitung, and the Parkview in Hualien. In Taipei, our home hotel was AMBA Ximending where we spent 17 nights, but we also had a chance to attend seminar lectures and other special dinner events in Taipei at Howard Plaza Hotel, The Grand Hyatt, and Great Skyview Hotel.

I can imagine my colleagues back home and those at the U. S. Department of State saying, "Surely, this poem and its subject cannot be evidence of serious academic scholarship. Even older brother, upon receiving the poem via text, said, "I think it's about time for you to come home."

Still, the poem does fit in the ancient literary tradition of scatological satire composed by authors such as Aristophanes, Chaucer, Rabelais, and my favorite, Jonathan Swift.

Composition. The most frequent question I received from friends and family about Taiwan was some form of "Do you think that China will invade soon?" I usually responded with a version of "I don't think I'll be vaporized while I'm there. I doubt the State Department would allow us to visit if there was any imminent threat of global conflict."

Of course, I have no idea when and if China will try some form of its Hong Kong strategy on Taiwan, but I'd also say that Taiwan is not Hong Kong or even Ukraine. For another thing, the Taiwanese pop-ulation has a long history of resilience and adaptation in the face of one invader or another.

It's also true that the U.S. has substantial economic, political, educational, and military relationships with Taiwan, plus the world's most valuable semiconductor manufacturing company TSMC is located in Taiwan. Also known as Taiwan's "Silicon Shield" against invasion, TSMC fabricates about 90 percent of the most advanced chips designed by U.S. semiconductor companies Apple, Google, Intel, AMD, Qualcomm, and Nvidia.

But this poem, the last one I composed, is more about the people of Taiwan and their history of resilience, symbolized most clearly for me in Taipei 101, as well as their featherlight agility and creative ability (even under existential threat from China) to absorb and transform that history into a new kind of democracy that seems to me to have generated significant success in respect, hope, security, and freedom in a very short period of time.

Images. The photo cover is by Ray Mikell, another member of the Fulbright-Hays Taiwan trip with me. As I was sharing these poems with our group, he was also sharing his wonderful photographs. Although a political science professor at Mississippi's Jackson State University, Ray Mikell has long maintained an interest in photography. He spent many years volunteering and serving as a writer on projects of the New Orleans Photo Alliance, a fine arts nonprofit. He has had photos in juried exhibits including a 2016 New Orleans Jazz and Heritage Festival focus on music of the American South.

Laurence Musgrove is a Fulbright-Hays Taiwan Seminar Scholar and teaches literature, composition, and creative writing at Angelo State University in San Angelo, Texas. His research focuses on effective pedagogy in teaching writing and literature, manifested most recently in "A Buddhist Educator's Perspective on Well-Being Across the Curriculum," Educator Perspectives. 1.1, 34-41.

His poetry appears in a wide range of journals in the U.S. and his three books *Local Bird, The Bluebonnet Sutras,* and *A Stranger's Heart,* all from Lamar University Literary Press. Laurence has also edited collections of creative writing, including *Texas Weather, Lone Star Poetry,* and *The Senior Class: 100 Poets on Aging.* He is also editor of the online journal Texas Poetry Assignment which publishes poems on Texas-related themes, sponsors online and area readings, and supports hunger relief in the state.

*9 7 9 8 8 9 9 9 0 1 1 9 5 *